A NEW DIMENSION
OF FREEDOM

Also by
LE GRAND E. DAY
Outline of the Theory of Multigovernment
and
A Letter From the Future

A New Dimension of Freedom

LeGrand E. Day

MOJAVE BOOKS • Reseda, California

ISBN 0-87881-064-1

Book design by Zvi Erez

PRINTED IN THE UNITED STATES OF AMERICA

MOJAVE BOOKS
7040 Darby Avenue
Reseda, California 91335

To the memory of my father,
Delbert E. Day.

PREFACE

I have written notes, outlines, and syllabuses on Multigovernment since the idea came to me in 1967. They have been Xeroxed, mimeographed, hectographed, and printed twice. They were originally designed for teaching in experimental colleges and for giving lectures on Multigovernment.

Only two were copyrighted: "Outline of the Theory of Multigovernment," in 1969, and "A Letter From the Future," in 1975.

The reason for bringing out the book at this time is the urgings of persons interested in Multigovernment to have something printed on the subject, and also there are other writers entering the field using many of my basic concepts and ideas.

The only major change in the theory of Multigovernment from the earlier writings is the concept that the echelon above the Geographical Democracy is a Judicial Republic and not a "confederation of world states," as first recorded. Much thought and study on the subject convinced me that beyond the basic local government, man does not have to be governed at all. Of course, he may join any choice government voluntarily.

The method of explaining Multigovernment, other than verbal description, has been going over and over in my mind for the last eight years. I am finding it difficult, with my limited capacity, to be technically correct and at the same time to make it understandable and interesting to the average reader.

The book will be a beginning, outlining the general format. In the future, I will clear up misunderstandings, perfect the method and description, and answer the critics of Multigovernment.

LET IT BE CLEARLY UNDERSTOOD THAT THIS
SYSTEM MUST WORK AND GROW WITHIN THE LEGAL
MEANS OF THE ALREADY-ESTABLISHED GOVERN-
MENTS. THE TOOLS NEEDED TO BRING ABOUT MULTI-
GOVERNMENT ARE COMMUNICATIONS, NOT BLOOD-
SHED; EDUCATION, NOT VIOLENCE; PERSUASION,
NOT REVOLUTION. THERE IS NOTHING IN THIS
THESIS THAT ADVOCATES, SUGGESTS, OR IMPLIES
THE OVERTHROW OF ANY EXISTING GOVERNMENT
BY FORCE OR VIOLENCE.

— *Le Grand E. Day*
Sunland, California
May, 1977

FOREWORD

Multigovernment will present to every individual the right to expand the choice of options in every aspect of his lifestyle. It will introduce a new dimension of freedom not yet experienced by mankind.

Not only is Multigovernment workable, but with the advent of sophisticated atomic weapons, it is necessary to save civilization as we know it.

TABLE OF CONTENTS

A NEW DIMENSION
OF FREEDOM

Chapter 1

Introduction

NEED FOR A CHANGE

Simply because an institution, a custom, or a social condition exists, its existence or its acceptance does not make it the right, the best, or the only choice.

That vague identity called the state (that indivisible chain that holds people together like ants or bees), in a modern world, exists for apparently two fundamental reasons: (1) to give continuity to its own existence, and (2) to maintain order and discipline.

The criteria to obtain leadership or for upward mobility in the state or any of its protected institutions suggests the possession of talents with questionable ethics. The political system itself is neither fair nor equitable.

Other than a long, slow process, there are only two ways to change the nature of the state: by invasion from another state or by revolution from within.

I suggest, without enlarging upon the inadequacies of the existing states, that if the members of society believe that they have the best alternative, they are naive and uninformed.

To change a system that will self-destruct in time anyway would be an act of mercy and compassion. But to disintegrate a system you already have, you must replace it with something better. Through evolution, not revolution, we introduce and suggest a change to a superior system: *Multigovernment.*

PHILOSOPHY OF MULTIGOVERNMENT

Multigovernment believes that the only legitimate purpose of a compulsory government is to provide adequate protection (fire and police) and fair and enforceable judgments.

Multigovernment also believes that each individual should have the opportunity to have as much freedom as he desires, without the infringement of others. It is obvious, without argument, that each individual's wants and desires are different.

Multigovernment therefore suggests that society should cater to man's differences by allowing the creation of many or multigovernments, to not subdue him to a mythical norm, an average, or one government — and this one government expected to be all things to all people.

It is, therefore, proposed that a new political system be introduced, and we suggest that it replace the present power structure.

GEOGRAPHICAL DEMOCRACY: Multigovernment suggests there be one compulsory government for each land area. It should be divided by population density and the will of the people. City-states should be created in metropolitan areas. City-states will replace city, county, state and, eventually, federal government. Territorial governments will grow in the farming, rural and forest areas, also replacing the above overlapping governments.

Multigovernment suggests it is only logical that, since all people living in the specified area must belong to this government, it be a democracy! Complying with the doctrine of Multigovernment, any services offered by this government other than those of geographical necessity should be voted on by 85 percent of all registered voters.

All policies instituted by local government should be voted on by the eligible voters. Only those operational decisions should be exempt from majority rule. Democracy must prevail by the nature of the government itself at this echelon of Multigovernment.

JUDICIAL REPUBLIC: The compulsory echelon above the geographical democracy in the Multigovernment system is not a government; that is, it does not govern. Multigovernment selected the name "Judicial Republic." It works as follows: There will be a pyramid of courts with judges at each level. On the bottom will be the local and regional courts and judges housed with, but not connected with, the local geographical governments. The chain then continues through the appellate court, supreme court (suggested for each continent), and finally to the upper supreme court.

The method of selecting judges should be a matter of policy as well as division of work. For instance, it might be practical to have one appellate court for individual rights, another for disputes among choice governments (yet to be explained), and one for criminal justice, etc. The number of judges at each level should also be a policy matter.

The judges themselves should adhere to the criteria of fairness and follow the doctrine of Multigovernment in matters of governmental dispute. Judges themselves should make policy concerning the structure and running of the judicial republic with a workable people's initiative for checking purposes.

CHOICE GOVERNMENTS

The *choice government* concept is the backbone of Multigovernment systems. Our descriptions up to this point have been of compulsory organizations; that is, the citizens have to belong to the geographical democracy and be subject to the rulings of the judicial republic. It is a philosophy of Multigovernment that when governments are compulsory, only those government functions absolutely necessary should be performed.

Compensating for the vacuum of services not performed by traditional government, Multigovernment suggests that governments be created to meet the different needs of men, so any man can find the exact, or almost perfect, government for him. Man, if he so desires, may belong to no government at all except the above compulsory governments with the bare necessary functions. Those who belong to no government are called "free agents."

The free agents will be living as the conservative (right-winger, libertarian, etc.) would like to live today; that is, conforming to their idea of freedom: freedom from government intervention. The weakness of present-day conservatism is that they do not take into account those who cannot exist, or do not wish to exist, in the conservatives' version of freedom.

On the other side of the coin, the weakness of liberalism (left wing, collectivism, etc.) is that they all want government services but in different ways. In other words, what, where, who, and how much? Each faction has its own idea about which direction government should go. The crux of the Multigovernment idea is that governments and organizations coexist and fulfill each faction's idea of good government. Then each person can choose from among the competitive governments, the government he wants to belong to.

Multigovernment will present to every individual the right to a broader choice of options in every aspect of his lifestyle. It will introduce a new dimension of freedom not yet experienced by mankind.

Multigovernment will eliminate wars. If government's ideology is built around the individual and not land-mass occupation, who are the conquerors going to conquer?

The Multigovernment system will cause all revolutions to cease. If you don't like the government you have, you can quit and join another.

Multigovernment makes the observation that no one system or form of government is best for all people. One

Chapter 2

The Basis of the Theory of
Multigovernment

The theory of Multigovernment envisions the creation of coexisting governments within the confines of existing countries. Governments will exist for their function — serving people — not by virtue of the fact that they occupy land mass. These coexisting sovereigns, motivated by competition, will represent the most efficient organizations devised by man.

Theory is defined as a direction of action based on principles verified by observation and thought. Each group of individuals has common concepts that hold them together. All states are guided by a political theory. The fact that a theory has never been developed, or accepted, is obviously no criterion that it will not work.

The theory of Multigovernment is based on six principles:

1. Each man's desires and needs for government are different.

2. The individual is capable of deciding for himself his own desires and needs.

3. Where man lives (geographical boundaries) should not be the determining factor of what government he should belong to.

4. Various governments can, and ought to, coexist in the same location.

5. Governments compete for membership with services, economies, or ideologies.

6. If he chooses, a man may belong to no government at all, accepting only the basic protection of the local community.

PRINCIPLE 1: EACH MAN'S NEEDS AND DESIRES FOR
A GOVERNMENT ARE DIFFERENT

The fact that each man has different needs and desires for government is a foregone conclusion. Each man is different by background, religion, language, culture or heritage; different by chance or different by choice. The world is already a multidiversified society, with numerous cultures and subcultures. It is undesirable — in fact, impossible — to mold the entire world into one culture, one religion, or even one country.

Behavioral scientists have made impressive advances, including the research and utilization of the principles of classification and stratification of peoples. These demographic concepts have been exploited by merchants all over the globe.

Government has also capitalized on this research. Government, however, has not considered how best it can serve, but how effectively it can persuade, manipulate, and control people.

As the worldwide trend moves to ever-increasing and advancing social legislation, discontent grows because of the diversified and individualized nature of mankind.

Individuals who rebel against these social changes fall in two basic categories:

1. Those who neither desire nor appreciate these changes and are capable of living in peace and happiness without them.

2. Those who want extra government benefits that are of a different nature or quantity than those offered by the state.

Any government that wishes to exist in the future must take into consideration these characteristics of humanity and compensate for it. The purpose of the existence of government is to serve people. The government should adjust to the people, not the people to the government.

Multigovernment offers an effective solution to the individual difference problem.

PRINCIPLE 2: THE INDIVIDUAL SHOULD DECIDE FOR HIMSELF THE GOVERNMENT HE WANTS TO SERVE HIM

Due to the superior quality and quantity of education, the world is enjoying the highest intellectual achievements in history. The masses are becoming enlightened and more aware of the social and political conditions. This superior knowledge enlarges the individual's ability to make rational political decisions. People are insisting on participating in the political decision-making process. Thus, knowledge becomes power.

Democracy exists in enlightened periods of world history because the backbone of democracy is the capability of people to understand the issues and to make intelligent judgments. Individuals are more qualified to decide what is best and good for themselves than are bureaucrats. The natural step in political evolution is from the majority deciding policy to the individual deciding his own policy.

Added to the freedoms, privileges, and rights man now enjoys, he is now responsible enough and willing enough to guide his own destiny.

Man has now intellectually advanced to the point that he should have the right to choose his own government.

PRINCIPLE 3: WHERE MAN LIVES (GEOGRAPHICAL BOUNDARIES) SHOULD NOT BE THE DETERMINING FACTOR OF WHICH GOVERNMENT HE BELONGS TO

Multigovernment suggests that land mass is not a legitimate claim or even a condition of national sovereignty. Political boundaries are unquestionably accepted by the population due to centuries of conditioning.

Some functions of government, by the nature of land-people relationship, must be performed by territorial government. However, most government functions can be performed better by people-oriented governments. It is ridiculous to assume that all phases of government administration must be administered by territorial government.

Every war that was ever fought, whatever the ideological excuse, was fought for land mass, and the national self-interest and power advantage the conquered territory offered the aggressor.

The fact that man must adhere to the policy of his government, whether he likes it or not, is the cause of all revolutions. Revolutions are bred by the assumption that every person born in a monarchy is a monarchist, in the boundaries of communism is a communist, and those in a socialist state adhere to the principles of socialism.

Civilization has now evolved to the point where political boundaries should be reevaluated. The legal claim to land mass is based on one or more of three conditions:

1. A piece of paper (treaties, constitutions, etc.)

2. Historical precedent

3. Status quo

These conditions assert that on one side of an imaginary line is one country, and on the other side is another country.

In the course of events, if a sovereign gains enough elements of power to overthrow his neighbor, all such legal claims become void. Then new papers are signed, another historical precedent created, and the status quo is changed. The stage is set for the drama to reenact itself in the future.

If man must group together — and some must — Multigovernment would suggest that it be done on the individual's own terms, be it ideological, religious, language, or even for ethnic reasons. Each individual should be allowed to choose, regardless of political boundaries, the type of government he wants to serve him.

Multigovernment offers man his natural right to choose his government, regardless of where he lives.

PRINCIPLE 4: GOVERNMENTS CAN, AND OUGHT TO, EXIST IN THE SAME LOCATION

Mankind must provide for himself the greatest individual potential growth by offering to his fellow man the largest possible variety of governments, so that he may exercise a broader option in his choice of government — one that fits his wants and needs.

The only feasible way this can be accomplished is to allow for many governments to exist in the same territory. These governments should be created with enough sovereignty to govern but without the power to compel.

Jewish kibbutzim, Catholic monasteries, and other organizations prove that tight organizations can exist on a volunteer basis within the established government. Many religious and fraternal societies, too numerous to mention, support the position that organizations can exist on a less militant basis.

There should be coexisting governments with various amounts of services offered, so that man may choose from among them the government he desires.

Multigovernment offers a logical basis where man can exercise his choice of government.

PRINCIPLE 5: GOVERNMENTS COMPETE FOR MEMBER-
SHIP WITH IDEOLOGY, ECONOMIES, OR
SERVICES

Competition, man's greatest individual and collective growth factor, should be utilized to create better governments as it has been used to make better automobiles, moon shots, and soccer teams.

The motivation factor that would help to establish and maintain the best possible governments would be competition. The idea is to create fair government rivalry by allowing the several governments to compete for their constituents.

If man does not like the government he belongs to, he would have one of three choices:

1. Resign and join another government that fits his needs.

2. Resign and join no government at all.

3. Resign and create a government that will fit his needs.

Multigovernment utilizes competition — man's greatest expansion factor.

PRINCIPLE 6: MAN MAY BELONG TO NO GOVERNMENT
AT ALL

In every culture, in every society, throughout the pages of history, there have existed those nonconformist, free, independent souls, called by some antisocial or rebellious individuals. These people provide mankind with most of the artists, writers, and thinkers. Impending social changes cramp their style, lessen their productivity, and make them miserable. These people, too, must live so that they are completely free except for basic protection of the law.

If a man so desires, he has a right to be free from all unnecessary governmental social enactments and restrictions.

Multigovernment offers more freedom than any existing government for those who really want it.

Governments will exist by virtue of the services they offer their constituency and how well they govern. In the past, governments existed by what the designs and accidents of history and geography have left them in the forms of land mass. For the first time in human history, governments will be created and stay in existence for the purpose of serving man.

Chapter 3

A New Dimension of Freedom

The individual in America is now burdened with four and sometimes more governments (i.e., town or city, county [or parish], state, and federal). All of these have cohesive and enforcement powers. This is a useless duplication of effort — a limitation of freedom.

Multigovernment suggests that only one territorial government be established for each area, hereinafter called "Territorial Governments." The boundaries of the Territorial Governments to be placed on the map in such a way as to allow for density of the population as well as the wishes of the inhabitants. This government will be responsible for police and fire protection.

To fill the vacuum of services now performed by the five governments, it is presupposed that a variety of organizations be created or existing governments be used for that purpose (service organizations, churches, etc.). These organizations will hereinafter be called "Choice Governments."

It is further presupposed that these Choice Governments will fall into four basic categories:

1. *Private Institutions* — Designed under the free enterprise system to meet the needs of the people.

2. *Special Districts* — Set up for a special service for which the individual only is taxed.

3. *Collective Governments* — Designed to give complete services, protection, and security for its members.

4. *Limited Governments* — To meet particular needs of certain persons.

If, for instance, an individual should choose the Collective Government (the third category), such as a kibbutz, a monastery or a socialist commune, he would probably not need the services of another government.

If, on the other hand, he should belong to a Limited Government furnishing only his housing, he could use the private institutions for his medical, his insurance, and a special district for his children to be educated, or he could send them to a parochial school.

A third individual could be completely free from all governments except the essential basics provided by Territorial Governments and belong to a Special District expressly designed for medical purposes.

It must be understood at this point that the so-called free enterprise system would prevail overall and the Choice Government would act as a unit in its dealings like a corporation. It is asserted that free individuals can live in the same geographical location as choice governments.

This should satisfy the individualist as he can live free from government intervention. This should satisfy the socialist-oriented person as he can belong to a socialist choice government. There will be a government or a set of governments that will satisfy everyone's exact needs or wants from government, and he will still belong to less than the five mandatory governments we now belong to.

The conservative will have his notion of freedom: free from all but necessary government functions. The collectivist will have his freedom from want in his choice of collective societies. The moderate, the religious man, etc., will all have their choices of government. There will exist a new dimension of freedom. Multigovernment believes the individual has the implied right to choose one's own government, whatever his geographical location.

Chapter 4

The Northridge Incident

The buildings of California State University, Northridge, were hazily silhouetted against the smoggy night. I left the Sierra Building and walked across the field where now stands the new library. I walked slowly and deliberately. Suddenly, in my scope of vision appeared a well-dressed man. I was slightly startled as he addressed me.

"Mr. Day?"

I did not answer him for a few seconds. I squinted my eyes toward him but did not recognize him. "Yes," I returned.

"You don't know me, but it's very important that we talk."

"I haven't much time. I work in the daytime and go to school at night. I need some sleep."

He went on as though he didn't hear me. "I am from another planet out of your universe. I have a message for the inhabitants of the earth."

My impression at this time was that he was being initiated for a fraternity.

"Come with me, please."

He gestured toward a large, circular, light-producing object that at that moment lighted up in the field. My impression then was that it was an elaborate joke to play. He must have had a lot of help from the Theatre Arts Department; the object was not there when the class started three hours ago.

Distance and depth have a way of playing tricks, and as we approached the illuminated object, I saw it was

17

bigger than I had originally supposed. It must have been
when I saw the men looking out the windows that I realized
it was indeed a space ship, and the man I was talking to
was a legitimate passenger. This realization became a
little frightening to me, so I stopped.

"Don't be afraid," the man said, "we won't hurt you."

"I am not afraid of being hurt," I said. "I am a bit appre-
hensive about something I know nothing about."

"We have important information to give you concerning
your world's present political system. We must insert a
new ideology or civilization because, as you know, this
system will be destroyed."

I have always been annoyed at the inadequate political,
social and economic state of the world. The thought of
something better intrigued me. The fascination of his
introduced subject matter seemed to overpower what fear
or apprehension I had.

We entered the space ship by a ramp that dropped down
from the side of the ship. When in the upper position, the
ramp was part of the exterior of the ship. There were steps
on the ramp, and as we entered a room that looked like
about a quarter of the ship, it was more like an office ante-
room than a space vehicle interior. I sat down in the last
remaining chair.

I felt a slight jerking, but it wasn't until I looked out of
the windows that I realized we were soaring away from
the earth.

"What's this important information you have for the earth?
Are you some kind of intergalaxy CIA or something?"

"No," he answered. "The system of government that
infects your planet will destroy your civilization if something is not done to change it. We selected you to convey
this message to the world."

"Why me?"

"We have selected you for three reasons: number one,
you are still a college student and responsive to new ideas;
number two, because of your age, your children are all

grown and you can devote full time to the changing of the system."

"Full time?" I exclaimed.

"Please let me continue," he went on. "And number three, you are a natural rebel, an agitator, and your psychological profile indicates that you can handle the assignment."

"Psychological profile!" I almost shouted. "I have a mania about my privacy," and at this point I was angered.

"Calm down, Mr. Day," he said patiently.

"How did you get a profile on me? Do you have access to the university records? What makes you think I will accept this so-called assignment? If you have been isolated from this planet for so many years, how can you speak English? Where do you come from, and who are you?"

"Take it easy, take it easy," he said. "We are now approaching the mother ship."

I saw out of the window a larger ship. The side of it opened and a hole appeared. The smaller ship entered the cavity formed by the opening and it seemed to fit snugly. The door that dropped down earlier from the smaller ship dropped down again. This time it opened to a room inside the larger ship. There were several chairs with adjustable writing boards, and a few men (apparently observers or witnesses or something) took the chairs in the back of the room and one chair was left for me. I sat down and adjusted the writing board.

I glanced around the room. It was kind of eggshell-colored. It reminded me of a cross between an Army Intelligence debriefing room and a college seminar classroom. As soon as I was seated, the man doing the talking left the room and another man entered. He sat in a chair without a writing board about fifteen feet in front of and facing me.

He was dressed differently from the others; he had on a brown form-fitting outfit with large pockets at hip length. His clothes looked like a modified jumpsuit. "Ah," I thought to myself, "a space man that looks like a space man."

"Good evening, Le Grand," he said. "My name is Dr. Peel."

This was the first time that my first name was used and the first time that anyone introduced himself.

"We are short of time. Let's get down to business."

"What's this assignment?" I asked.

"Perhaps 'assignment' was a bad choice of words. Let me tell you what we want you to do."

"Please do."

"To save your planet from almost sure destruction, we would like to outline a superior political system. You must take this basic structural form of government we will explain to you and introduce it into your literature and do whatever you can by way of teaching and lectures and, hopefully, curtail this disaster."

"Are you going to check on me for progress or reports, or something?" I remarked sarcastically.

"No," he said seriously. "This will be our last visit with you. Technically, we can't return until a few generations have passed."

"You'll return generations later?" I asked. "You mean, you live longer than we do?"

"Yes, our life-span is much longer. We must confine our discussion to political matters. It will be sufficient to say at this point, however, that there are other intelligences in the galaxy and other men with the same kind of bodies that you have. Each planet is at a different stage of development. The problem with your development is that something went wrong with your political growth and you advanced in the wrong direction."

"You said the political system will destroy itself. How will this be done?"

"What do you think could destroy your civilization?"

"The hydrogen bomb, or some other sophisticated war weapons," I guessed.

"Now remember, we are talking about political matters."

"In that case, it would be one country attacking another," I said.

"There are now 143 nations with sovereignty in the UN. Five of these have the hydrogen weapon. You have known from your own American experience that a head of state can become unstable. If just one of the leaders of these 143 countries gets access to the hydrogen bomb and uses it, it would cause a chain reaction that would destroy civilization. For instance, if Cuba or one of the small countries in Central America drops a bomb on the United States, it would be disastrous."

"You want to do away with countries? You want to get rid of nationalism?"

"Not exactly," Dr. Peel said. "Let's start at the beginning. Let's call this new governmental system 'Multigovernment.' It seems to best fit the word structure of your language. Now, to understand this system as you hear it the first time, you must erase from your mind the structure of your own American government and the structure of other governments you have studied in comparative government courses. We have the advantage to compare governments on different planets, and the outline we give you will be the synthesis of those governments that have worked best for other planets. Please be sympathetic and receptive to these new concepts that we present to you now, and trust us that it is a far superior system than you have."

"Okay, I am ready," I said as I put my notebook in place.

"Now the basic government is a geographical democracy. There are four prerequisites for this government. They are: (1) it must be a pure democracy in nature, (2) it must perform only the necessary governmental functions, (3) its boundaries must be flexible, and (4) it must have one government to each geographical area.

"All right, let's take the items one at a time. The first is that the geographical democracy must be a democracy. We see if a government is governing because it occupies land mass. That means that the people who live in the area covered by the government *must* belong to the government whether they like it or not. That means they must have maximum input into the system. Therefore, all compulsory governments must be democracies."

I said, "Democracies have too many basic weaknesses. Personally, I most strenuously object to the majority telling me what kind of government I am to have."

"Many others feel the same way," Dr. Peel said. "That brings us to item two; that is, only necessary government functions must be performed by the basic governmental unit or geographical democracy. By necessary government functions, we usually mean only fire and police protection."

"Good grief," I broke in. "Your basic governmental unit would be comparable to our city government, and our city governments handle such necessary things as parks, playgrounds, golf courses, garbage pickup, museums, and so on."

"These 'necessary things' are not as necessary as people think they are," Dr. Peel said. "Most of them can be taken care of by other organizations or governments or individuals. We would like you and other writers who write on Multigovernment in the future to substantiate this and other positions that we present to you. We must go on. We haven't much time.

"The third item," he continued, "is that the boundaries must be flexible. You must change your boundaries when the need arises."

"The reason the present boundaries are inflexible today is the difficulty of administrative changes along with the question of power," I said.

"That is why fire and police protection are the only services for the basic unit."

"If they are flexible, who is to decide where the boundaries are going to be?" I asked.

"The people," he said, as though I should know. "Your history is full of ridiculous boundary disputes and wars, when the answer is so obvious. Without question, without rebuttal, without discussion, when a boundary dispute arises, it must be voted on by the people living within the disputed boundaries. The people should have the opportunity to vote to be associated with any of the connected areas or to be a unit unto themselves."

"All right, I understand. When I get back home, I will give this some thought," I said.

"Now, for the last item of the prerequisites for geographical democracies," Dr. Peel went on. "There must be only one government for each area."

"You couldn't mean one government over the whole globe. We just talked about boundaries."

"No, no, no," Dr. Peel appeared annoyed at me. "There will be local units spaced all over the earth as we discussed before. They will be placed, taking into account the population (its density), economic conditions, special geographical considerations, and the moods of the people. We can assume that those living in large metropolitan areas will have the tendency to gather together into one geographical democracy. We call these city-states, the ones out in the rural farming and forest areas are called territorial governments. These are the two classes of geographical democracies. These local units usually evolute from cities and the counties of your phase of historical development. You understand now this important point, that this local unit government, or geographical democracies as we call them, will be replacing the city, the county, the state, and the federal governments."

"The *federal* government?" I emphasized the word "federal."

"Yes, the federal government," Dr. Peel repeated.

"Wait a minute," I said. "I believe and always believed that the federal government is a useless hunk of bureaucratic waste. But to do away with it completely would mean that I would be an anti-nationalist, or an internationalist. I am a good American, I spent eight years in the military service, I am patriotic and all that. I am a rebel, an agitator, and the other things the gentleman said, but I am not going to give my family the burden of having a

traitor in the family." At this point, I was upset and willing
to call the whole deal off.

"Hear me out," Dr. Peel broke in. "Nationalism is a
feeling of belonging. You do not have the expertise in
psychology to understand nor do we have the time to
explain, but this nationalism — or the feeling of being part
of something — can easily be transferred to choice governments, where the individual has the opportunity to be
associated with, and governed by, people of like nature,
background, and similar thinking. Nationalism, as you
know it, is simply gathering together people living in the
same geographical area. Under this new choice government system, nationalism would be even more pronounced
and precious for those types of people who need it."

"Choice governments," I asked, "what in the world are
they?"

"The big problem is that they are not in the world," he
quipped. "Let's get into choice governments. If only the
necessary functions are taken care of by geographical
democracies, then for those who want, need, or would
appreciate more government functions, who do you think
would perform them?"

"Choice governments, I suppose," I said.

"That is right. All of the people must belong to the local
unit. From that point on, they can choose from among the
thousands of governments that exist, the exact government
(or governments, in some cases), or no government at all.
This free choice of governments is a right of all citizens."

"Wait a minute. You said there was only one government
for each land area. Where are these choice governments
going to be?"

"They exist without land mass," Dr. Peel said. "Which
brings up a new point that your planet has made a mistake
about."

"What is that?" I asked.

"Your earth's leaders and theorists have made a very
important wrong assumption. Remember, JUST BECAUSE

SOME GOVERNMENT FUNCTIONS MUST HAVE A GEO-
GRAPHICAL BASE, ALL GOVERNMENT FUNCTIONS DO
NOT HAVE TO. This point, now, if you can grasp the concept, concludes that we can separate those functions (usually
of a protective nature) that are tied to land mass, from
those functions (usually human wants) that have nothing
to do with land mass. This separation can give the individual the right to choose the human functions he wants,
which is, in effect, choosing his own government. Let me
restate that."

"I get it," I said.

He began restating anyway. "Your planet has been
concerned with keeping the power elite in power, thereby
continuing the status quo. To satisfy the establishment
and their leaders, your theorists built their political theory
around a vague and useless strange agreement called
'social contract theory.' Neither the theorists nor the leaders
took into account human needs, desires and wants, so they
built government structure oriented toward keeping themselves in power. We would like to suggest strongly that
you replace the ridiculous 'social contract theory' with the
'individual contract theory,' which, in effect, states that
beyond the basic protective functions of the basic geographical democracy, each individual makes his own contract with his own government. Each individual has a
right to choose his own government no matter where he
lives, just as he has a right to choose his own lifestyle,
religion, insurance company, make of car, etc., etc."

"Let me understand what you are saying," I said. "If
this Multigovernment was in effect at this present time,
you mean I could belong to any government I wanted, still
living in the same place I now do? I could be a communist,
a nazi, a socialist, and my neighbor would have the same
choice?"

"Yes, these governments coexist simultaneously within
the same land area. Remember now, land area or land
mass is not a criteria for government," he said.

"What if I wanted to join another government while I was a member of the present one? In other words, if I changed my mind about the merits of my government, could I change governments?"

"Yes," he said.

"If you know so much about me, you will know that I am a libertarian, basically a conservative. I do not like government interfering in my business or interrupting my privacy. What about me, if I don't want any government at all?"

"You join no government at all, and you will be subject only to a geographical democracy," he answered.

"There was a time in my life," I continued, "when the church I belonged to was the most important thing in my life. If this happens again, would I be able to belong to my church?"

"Yes. Not only will you be able to belong to it, but if it was the most important organization in your life, you might belong to a church government or a theocracy."

"If there was no existing government that lived up to my idea of government, what would I do?"

"You could get together with people of like mind and create your own government," Dr. Peel answered. "Or there is another possibility. You could use the services of several governments if they agreed."

"What about my children if the government I belonged to didn't have any school system?"

"If the government you belong to doesn't have a school system, you can choose among the many private parochial and standard schools that are available."

"You have competing school districts as you have competing governments?" I asked.

"Yes, that is the crux of the system. Freedom and choice."

"Doesn't this make for a complicated mix-up and extra work?"

"No. Think about it for a while. A lot less problems than we have now. If you are a free agent, the only government that will have account for you and collect taxes is the geographical democracy. If you belong to only one government, you would have to pay taxes only to the two governments: the one of your choice and the geographical democracy. That would include almost all the people. As it is now, you must belong to city, county, state, federal, and whatever special district or school district that the power elite wants to assess."

"I can see one underlying weakness of the system," I said.

"What is that?" Dr. Peel responded.

"What would happen if one of the choice governments got enough power and wanted to take over a few other choice governments?"

"They would be checked by the integrated force of the judicial republic," he answered.

"Now I know you are expecting me to ask what is the integrated force of the judicial republic."

"Let's take the judicial republic," Dr. Peel went on. "This is the echelon above the geographical democracy notwithstanding the choice governments."

"Hold it," I said. "You said there were no governments you are expected to owe allegiance to except your choice government and the geographical democracies. Now you are giving me this judicial republic."

"The judicial republic is not a government; that is, it doesn't govern. It is a court system with enforcement power."

"Where does this integrated force come from? Are they a standing volunteer army?" I asked.

"No," he said. "They are recruited from the peace forces of the geographical democracies we talked about earlier. When there is a need for enforcement action, the judicial republic, under a court order, calls up the police forces of the local units that are not involved in the dispute to maintain order. When order is restored, or the need for mobilization is over, they return to their respective local units."

"Okay," I said. "Let's get back to this judicial republic you were talking about."

"Judicial republic is a system of courts. It starts with the local unit and pyramids up to different plateaus, the division of which is based on workload, type of cases, or value of cases. When it reaches what we call in most planets, the upper supreme court, they have the final say."

"How many people are there in the upper supreme court?" I queried.

"Usually three; in some planets there are more."

"Then these three people rule the world."

"No," he said emphatically. "Please understand it is a court function. They make judgments on actions, issues, and questions. They do not govern."

"Somebody has got to govern!" I almost shouted.

"No, that is another mistake your earth has made. At that level, no governing is necessary."

I staggered for a minute in thought. This concept crushed my chest like a hammer, but then I realized that he was right!

"We must get on, Mr. Day. You can look at your notes later."

"All right, all right. Let me clear my head. There are now federal and international functions of government that must still go on. I can see that if the entire world is Multi-government, there would be no need for a defense department. What about a defense department and a state department for other planets, and what about minting currency and distributing it, what about the postal system? I could go on and on."

"This concept is new to you, Mr. Day, but like the functions of the other governments (city, state, and county), they are not absolutely necessary. Defense is unnecessary between planets. Because of logistics, planets are too far apart to make invasion possible. The state department is unnecessary, obviously. The post office department is turned over to private industry and cooperatives. Now for the currency, welfare, and departments that have an ongoing nature. The judicial republic creates administrative districts and departments to administer these functions."

"They would be governments in and of themselves," I said.

"Yes, some observers refer to them as governments. They create districts for a specific problem or production. When the need for their services is over, then the district is discontinued. But the departments are of a continuous nature. They are reviewed yearly by the judicial republic (the judges). The departments adjust their personnel and operations to fit the findings of these reviews.

"It's almost time to leave now. Let me recap in a nutshell the overall theory of Multigovernment. Please remember that specific operating procedures and policies must be adjusted to particular locations, economic social conditions, and the moods of the people.

"The presumption of Multigovernment and the basis of its structure is that each individual must have the largest latitude humanly possible in either subjecting himself to a Multigovernment of his own choice or to be free. Also, that governments are to be oriented to serve man, not governed to serve the elite.

"The doctrine of Multigovernment is that there be at the geographical base a unit of limited powers called a geographical democracy. This geographical democracy covers the entire globe and is subdivided to best serve the inhabitants. There will be a judicial republic that has a court system from the base of the local government and reaches to a supreme court. These courts are charged with the responsibility of fair and honest judgment and the maintenance of the doctrine of Multigovernment. Any person born into this system will belong to the geographical democracy and be subject to the judgments of the judicial republic, but beyond that, he is absolutely free to choose."

When the session was over, I approached Dr. Peel, thinking perhaps a handshake or some customary parting gesture was in order. But Dr. Peel faded away. The messenger suggested it was time to leave.

We reversed the entrance procedure. As we were returning to earth, in the satellite, my mind was pulsating between the technical aspects of the flight and the political philosophy. I finally broke the silence.

"How am I, one man, going to get across to the entire world this 'Multigovernment'?"

"Your first job will be to get down on paper the basic concepts of this philosophy. Then work out a system of government based on the basic philosophy best suited to your time and planet."

"Is that all?"

"No. You must spend the rest of your life doing basically two things: One, write, lecture, and teach the basic concepts of Multigovernment; and two, use what resources you have and what talents you can muster to publicize and advertise this superior system of government."

"What do you mean, the remainder of my life?" I exclaimed. "I have other plans."

"Think about it seriously. It would take one hydrogen bomb from one well-meaning, misguided dictator, and your planet would experience the biggest holocaust in history, and civilization as you know it would be destroyed."

"It is a big responsibility."

"As proven by other planets, when you get started, intelligent people will see the situation realistically and embrace your alternative and help you in two ways. One, by writing literature supporting the theory of Multigovernment, and two, by providing leadership in the movement designed to bring about Multigovernment."

By that time the plane had landed.

"I have a million more questions," I said.

"You have had enough information on the political system. If you are curious about the technical aspects of the flight and our civilization as others have been, it is not our mission nor do we have time to explain."

The door opened and the messenger directed me to it. "Good luck, Mr. Day."

He then held his hands above his head, fingers extended, and thrust his hands toward me, saying loudly:

"MULTIGOVERNMENT."

This gesture has become a symbol of Multigovernment movements by crowds in unison, or as a parting gesture of two MGs (usually only one hand thrust forward when an individual was leaving another individual).

I was deposited on the grass where I was picked up, and I watched the airship take off with its one main light and watched the light as it got smaller and smaller as it soared through the sky.

It finally lit up the night about as much as the stars for about half a minute, then it disappeared from sight. The next day's local paper read, "UFO SIGHTED ON NORTHRIDGE CAMPUS."

Chapter 5

A Letter from the Future

"A Letter from the Future" is a method to simplify the description of the theory on Multigovernment and make it more understandable. It is not designed as an exercise to predict or prophesy the future.

This method is not new, Sir Thomas More used his hypothetical island "Utopia." Francis Bacon had his "new Atlantis" to picture his ideal commonwealth. Tomasina Campanella utilized a heavenly "City of the Sun."

I am using somewhat the same method of Edward Bellamy and George Orwell by moving across the face of time.

Title: A Letter from the Future

From: Ernest Yad
         California State University, Northridge
         City-State Los Angeles

Date: July 4, 2176

To: Inhabitants of the 20th Century

I am a college student, majoring in English with an emphasis on the language and colloquialism of the 20th Century. My Master's project is to write a letter to the people living around July 4, 1976 (America's Bicentennial). This thesis will give the history of the interceding two hundred years between 1976 and 2176. It will briefly describe the political system. I will proceed to write as I am writing directly to the people of the 20th Century.

I have selected to write to the last quarter of the 20th Century because you are living in a time of an interesting paradox. You are now celebrating the courage and foresight of those who lived two hundred years before you (1776), having no idea that History would record your time as the lowest ebb in American history.

However, out of the corruption and chaos of the 1970s came the seeds of a new political system that, in sixty years, would be the determining ideology of a continent. It would circle the earth before the century was over. The system was called, in your day, "Multigovernment." In our day, it is the natural, permanent ethos. It is our way of life. It is as superior to your system as yours is to slavery.

California State University, Northridge, California, retained its name between your 20th Century and my 22nd Century. This was done to honor the birthplace of Multigovernment in 1969. However, the identity of the State of California has disappeared.

Multigovernment was first organized by L. E. Day, then developed by others. It was expanded on street corners and in experimental colleges. It started with mimeographing machines and graduated to printing presses. The movement was spearheaded by young college students and the so-called underground. They realized that the conservative-liberal pull would be the stagnation of civilization unless a system was devised giving each individual his natural right to choose his own form of government.

(If you are reading this around 1976, why don't you look up the Multigovernment Publications and Lecture Bureau and be part of history?) The bureau was a cadre of workers for Multigovernment. It soon evoluted into a political party in the Southern California area.

MGs, as the Multigovernment political party became known, appeared on the California ballot in 1985. The political party spread from California (a fertile soil for germinating ideas) to the entire globe. MG soon became a political movement in every country on earth where it was legal.

The Middle East, a traditional conflict area of the world, took the first giant step toward Multigovernment. Israel, Samaria, Jordan, and the Gaza Strip were made into one republic. The land was split up among the several states. The territory was divided to best maximize the population among the various ethnic groups. The Jewish majority had overall leadership and took up the land area not covered by the various states. The Jews handled such matters as foreign affairs, currency, and defense; the rest of the member states having their own courts, police force, schools, medical and other services.

The next logical step was to have the first experiment in Multigovernment. It happened in 1995. The Jewish majority made themselves into a sovereignty without territory. They also made the several states into a sovereignty without land. Other governments were created according to the various religious, ethnic, or philosophical notions. The people then had the right to choose the government they wanted. Some people decided to get together with others of like ideology and create a government according to their own particular specifications. Each individual also had the right to belong to no government at all.

The world then had its first working model of Multigovernment. The Israeli-Palestine showcase spurred the growth of MG parties throughout the world.

On August 10, 2012, our "Fourth of July," Australia became the first continent to accept the Multigovernment system as a total political existence. The time period between the beginning of Multigovernment in 1969 and the freedomization of the first continent in 2012 was historically called the "persuasion period."

The next three decades, known as the "transition period," was a test for Multigovernment. It was a conflict between two factions: not communism and capitalism as so many had predicted, but between the bulky land-mass sovereigns and Multigovernment.

Country after country joined the ranks of the superior system. The rapid growth of Multigovernment put stress on the system. As a result, anti-freedom forces tried to recapture the land controlled by Multigovernment. Most of the people, by this time, were college graduates. They not only could have the advantage of the historical perspective on which was the better system, but they also could make a comparative analysis. During the transition period, both systems simultaneously coexisted.

Freedomization of the world came about in 2045 when Madagascar, the last holdout, became part of Multigovernment. This ended the transition period that started when Australia entered the system.

The millenium was ushered in on March 16, 2076, when the entire world agreed to a constitution with the concept of Multigovernment as its basis. Since there were no wars, no violence, no revolutions, this period gets little space in history books. When the millenium started, there were no wars because there was no land mass controlled by governments to fight for. There were no revolutions because if you didn't like the government you belonged to, you could quit and have three options: (1) join another government, (2) join no government at all, or (3) create your own government.

Land is a place you live in and travel on. Government is a device to serve people. What we cannot understand in our time about the people of your time is why you cement the two together simply because some government functions need a geographical base.

We will now examine the present political condition. The doctrine of Multigovernment, which is basically the same today, was taught back in the 20th Century. The broad framework of political theory was called Multigovernment. However, some aspects have changed. These changeable things we call "policy." Policy is those aspects of government that change with people's moods, wants, and conditions at a particular time and place. However, the basic theory of Multigovernment contained in the writings of L. E. Day and others allows for the fluctuations of policy.

We will now look at an overview of the political system we have today that grew out of the 20th Century Multigovernment (MG). We have three echelons of government that need explaining at this time: (1) territorial, (2) judicial, and (3) choice.

There is only one territorial government in Multigovernment to each land area, and each land area has only one territorial government. (The above apparent repetition is intentional because of prior misunderstanding on this point.) The theory suggests that only these problems of "territorial necessity" be handled by the territorial government. If there is any function other than police or fire protection (which is a territorial necessity), it must be voted on by 85 percent of the entire voting public of the geographical area. The idea is to keep the territorial government at a bare minimum. By the nature of the fact that all the people that live in them must belong to them, all territorial government must be democracies.

City-states have formed in large metropolitan areas
and heavily populated areas. Regional governments have
formed in rural, farming, and forest areas.

The judicial level of government's basic function is the
court system. The judicial system does not actually govern—
they judge. However, as will be taken up later, they appoint
districts or departments to administer. The judicial system starts with the local courts, seeming to be on the level
with, and housed with, territorial governments, then
stretches out to the district courts, regional courts, the
supreme court for each continent, and then an upper
supreme court.

The method of judges getting their positions is a policy
matter and is changed through the years. At the present
time, one third of the judges are appointed by the territorial
officials who are elected by the people (indirect representa-
tion), one third are elected by the people (direct election),
and the last one third are appointed by the original two
thirds (appointments).

The administrative districts and departments are sometimes called a level of government, but they are usually
considered under our court system. The administrators
follow policy set by the courts.

This type of subgovernment is divided into two categories:
departments and districts. Departments are permanent
and handle things that are of an ongoing nature such as
currency, welfare, etc. Districts are of a temporary, *ad hoc*
nature and disband when the function they perform can
be handled by another form of government by individuals,
or there is no longer a need for their goods or services.

The choice government aspect of our system is the backbone of Multigovernment theory. A definition of choice
government, for our purposes at this time, is a government
where the individual can choose, from among the several
governments, one to fulfill his human needs. The individual's protection needs are filled by the geographical
government. His judicial needs are filled by the judicial

government. Two conditions must exist for the choice government concept to work: (1) the system must provide an atmosphere so the choice governments can be created and grow by their merits, and (2) there must be people ready to start and maintain choice governments. Both of these conditions exist today and the system is working beautifully.

The idea or concept of man's basic organizational needs was first taught by MGs back in your day, and today has proven to be true. Man's organizational needs fall into three basic categories: (1) those who have a tendency toward leadership; (2) those who have a tendency toward following, and (3) those who do not need to either lead or follow. In most societies, before Multigovernment this condition of man's organization deviation was not taken into account. Today, because of our many choice governments that exist for men to choose from, each of these needs that a man has can be fully satisfied.

In the Multigovernment system, individuals have an opportunity to express their natural and acquired talents. As far as political and social experimentation is concerned, it offers a very important opportunity for experiments in government. Prior to Multigovernment, experimental governments had to come about with bloody revolutions or expensive educational programs.

Today, we have a large range of governments from which to choose. We have a choice ranging from local regional-based organizations to large world cooperation. We can choose from ethnic-oriented governments to multi-race fellowships. Or our choice can range from loose democracies to strict disciplined societies (every person has the right to leave the choice government he belongs to at any time). In the last one hundred years, every possible form of government conceived by the minds of men has existed. Those survived which best fulfilled the needs of the people. These are needs that people of your generation completely ignored.

Our political scientists and organizational theorists have categorized choice government into many forms. The most popular form is a structural form. They are listed in four categories: (1) limited government, (2) religious or ethnic government, (3) comprehensive government, and (4) free agents (free agents are not a form of government but they must be accounted for).

It so happens that my three roommates at the college (Larry, Bruce, and Chris) and I all belong to one of the above categories. I will very briefly describe each of my roommates' governments so that the reader can get a rough idea of how the governments work today.

I belong to a Socialist Democratic Government. We are located close to the center of population in the Antelope Valley next to a city-state of Los Angeles. We are a farming and food-producing government. We hold all things in common. We have a college dedicated to the improvement of agriculture and food-producing. I was not interested in the processing of food, so my government sent me to California State University, Northridge, to study English.

Restating a principle of Multigovernment, land is not a prerequisite for government, but because of the purpose of our government (which is to raise food), we own our own land in the same way as individuals and corporations did in your day and still do in our day. We all own the government's land collectively. If anyone wishes to join a new government or be independent (a free agent), we give him a prearranged portion of money or goods.

We use the barter system within the governments when they have a product or service. We trade food with them. For instance, we exchange food for medical care with the government that specializes in hospitals and medical care. California State University, Northridge, was turned over to an educational district many years ago, and my government has made arrangements with that district for the education of those college students from our government who are not interested in agriculture.

My government takes pride in the amount of food we produce. We feel good when we allocate a portion of food to governments that are not as fortunate as ours, much like the volunteer system advocated by the Libertarian Party of your day.

I could go on and give you an in-depth analysis of our government's method of democracy, its organizations, its history, etc., but I will confine this description to its relationship with other governments and individuals. It is hoped that the reader can conceive the broad picture of how the system works.

My roommate Larry belongs to a religious society as an example of the religious and ethnic category. He belongs to one of the two largest religions that existed in your day and still exists today. His father works for a regular business corporation. He gives a portion of his salary to the church. He owns his own home, and his medical expenses are paid by the company he works for, through insurance. All of the remaining government's functions are taken care of by his church, including taking care of the old and those who cannot work.

Now again, there are religious societies which do nothing but answer to the religious needs of the people, and there are those which are comprehensive; that is, they take full responsibility for their members from cradle to grave.

My roommate Chris belongs to the Granite Dual Republic, to be used as an example of limited government. It is called Dual because it has only two areas of government: medical needs and education. So, individuals who belong to the Granite Dual Republic do not have any other type of government except the basic protection of the geographical community government services and, of course, they are subject to the judicial system. About half the people of the Granite Dual Republic work full time for the government; that is, they teach in the schools, work as doctors, or are in related occupation or crafts. The other half works outside the organization and pays taxes for its services.

The Granite Dual Republic, like my government, trades its hospitalization and school services with other governments that have services or products to trade, such as our government trades food produced by our people for medical services performed by their people. They also sell these services to free agents and others whose governments do not provide them.

My last roommate is Bruce, whose parents are free agents. That is, they belong to no government at all. They, of course, belong to the local community and are subject to the judicial system. But other than that, they are completely free from government intervention. The children of free agents are subject to the educational voucher system until they get through high school. That is, the children and the parents of school-age free agents can choose a parochial school, a school district school, or a government school when there is an opening and when the governments of the school districts can handle them.

Everyone in our society is guaranteed a free education through college. Free agents are the biggest single group. Free agents are living as the conservative, the libertarian, or the right-winger wanted to live in your day. They live completely their notion of freedom, without government intervention or interference except for the bare necessities.

The reason the believers in Multigovernment in the 20th Century were associated with the conservative movement is that they both had the same basic objectives in mind.

What difference did it make to the true conservative if his neighbor belonged to a cooperative or a socialist form of government as long as he, himself, was free? That was to provide for those who could not make it or did not want to work in a free society.

Now in the case of the liberal or left-winger, each wanted to go in a different direction or have a different amount of government services, each liberal demanding that the entire government be oriented toward his brand of liberalism.

So, dear reader, political life as you live it is the right pulling against the left. If you don't end up with one suppressing the other, you end up with a coalition, which is nothing. You are now in a historical persuasion period. Perhaps you have thought about history and wondered why the serf of the Middle Ages, without question, subjected himself to a lord of the manor when freedom was just over the hill. We have wondered why the slaves of any time period stayed with their masters when freedom was so close. We here in the 22nd Century look back to you of the 20th Century and ask with the same concern, "Why do you keep those, without question, those wasteful, useless governments?"

Chapter 6

Method of Implementation

A political theory is written with a condition, a hope, and a dream.

The condition: that the theory be published and have a fair hearing. The hope: that men who believe in its concepts will create organizations to perpetrate its growth. The dream: that mankind will see its superiority and accept it as a permanent ethos.

The Multigovernment Society was created to accomplish the above hope. Members have been nicknamed "MGs." The Multigovernment Publications and Lecture Bureau was established to perform the two services mentioned in its title, and to recruit leadership, and to provide doctrinal format for the society.

When you read this book, give it careful thought, study, and prayer. If you realize, as many others have, that Multigovernment or something like it must prevail or civilization as we know it will be destroyed, and you wish to add your talents to the Society, we welcome you.

Multigovernment Publications and Lecture Bureau
P. O. Box D D
Sunland, California 91040

GLOSSARY

It became apparent in early writings of Multigovernment that a glossary was necessary. These terms are used when discussing and describing Multigovernment and do not necessarily conform to any dictionary definition or any other criteria.

1. ADMINISTRATIVE DISTRICT. A government district created, controlled, and periodically reviewed by the judicial republic to perform functions of government that cannot be handled by choice governments, geographical governments, or individuals.

2. CHOICE GOVERNMENTS. A noncompulsory government where individuals choose for themselves the backbone of Multigovernment.

3. DAYISM. A term used to describe Multigovernment; we prefer Multigovernment.

4. DOCTRINE (of Multigovernment). Doctrine is considered permanent concepts of Multigovernment; i.e., geographical democracy, judicial republic, etc.

5. FREEDOMIZATION. A term used in "A Letter from the Future," meaning the acceptance of land areas by Multigovernment.

6. GEOGRAPHICAL DEMOCRACY. Along with the judicial republic, the only government that is compulsory. It is Multigovernment doctrine that three conditions exist for geographical democracies: (1) one geographical democracy covers each area; (2) geographical democracies are pure democracies; (3) whenever possible, the services are kept down to protective functions (geographical necessity).

7. GEOGRAPHICAL NECESSITY. Geographical necessities are those necessary functions of government that must be performed by the geographical democracy.

8. INDIVIDUAL CONTRACT THEORY. In contrast to the social contract theory, Multigovernment suggests that each individual make his own contract with the government.

9. INTEGRATED FORCE. The enforcement agency of the judicial republic. They are temporary and are recruited from geographical democracy's police forces. They are used for peace-keeping missions, and when the crisis or reason for their recruitment is over, the force returns to the duty of police force of the various geographical democracies.

10. MILLENIUM. The millenium is the historical period of Multigovernment when the entire world comes under this system.

11. OPERATIONAL DECISIONS. Decisions made by the geographical democracies and the administrative districts that are related to operative procedures. These decisions do not have the magnitude to be reviewed by the judicial republics in the case of administrative districts or to be voted on by the people in the case of the geographical democracies.

12. PERSUASIAN PERIOD. A political historical period starting in 1969 and ending when the first country adopted Multigovernment.

13. POLICY. Policy is issues and operating procedures that change with the times, places, economic conditions, and the moods of the people. It is in contrast to doctrine that is inflexible and stays the same.

14. PURE DEMOCRACY. Pure democracy is a type of democracy that describes the geographical democracy

wherein all policy and issues are voted on by the people. Only minor operational decisions are not voted on.

15. RELATIVE DOCTRINE.   Relative doctrine means such concepts, ideas, issues or policies that are directly related to Multigovernment. Such things as gun control laws, abortion, etc., are not relative doctrine. Although each individual has a right to his own opinion, the Multigovernment Publications and Lecture Bureau does not take a stand on issues unless they are of relative doctrine.